Deciduous Forest

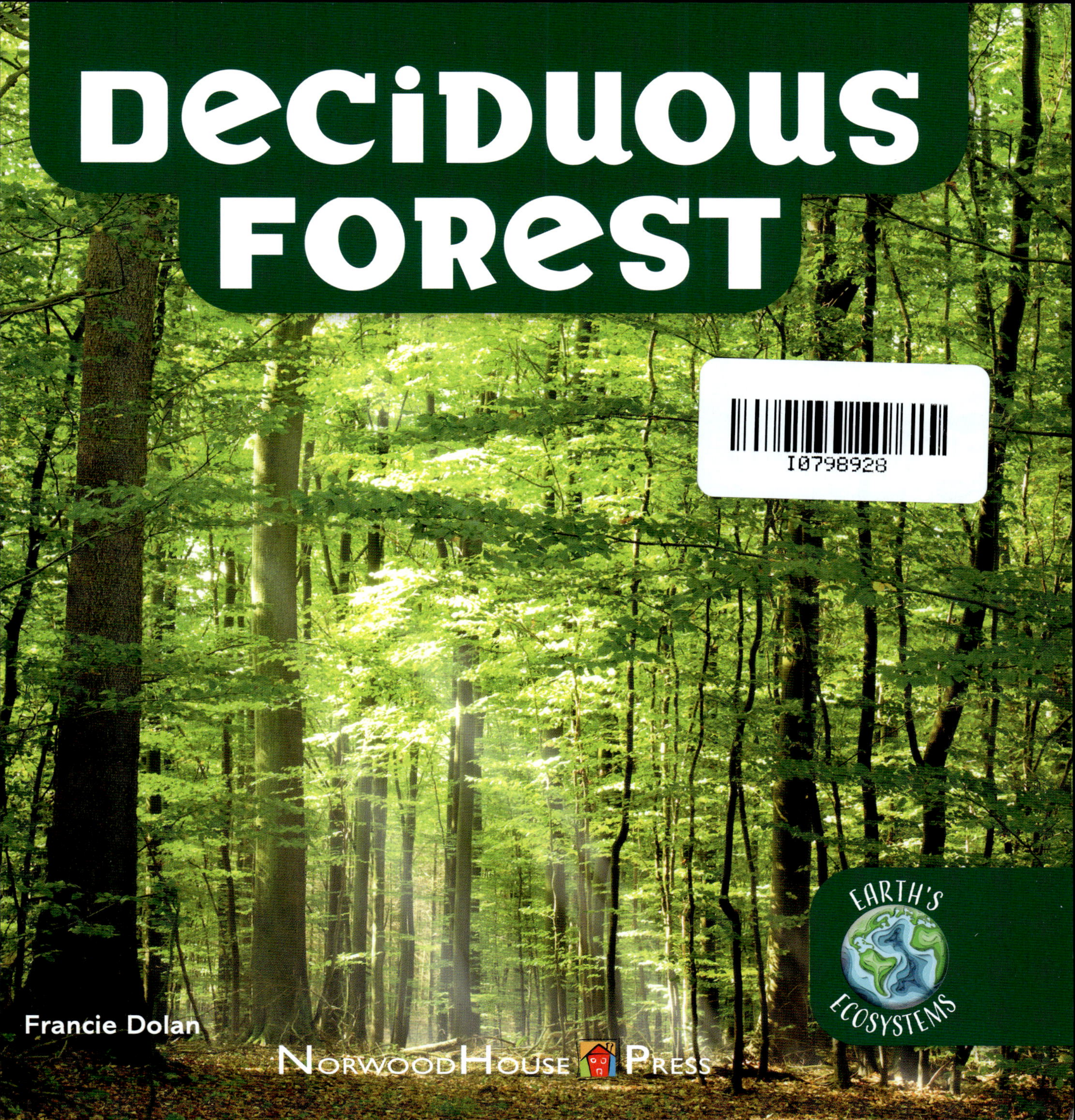

Earth's Ecosystems

Francie Dolan

Norwood House Press

Cataloging-in-Publication Data

Names: Dolan, Francie.
Title: Deciduous forest / Francie Dolan.
Description: Buffalo, NY : Norwood House Press, 2026. | Series: Earth's ecosystems | Includes glossary and index.
Identifiers: ISBN 9781978577138 (pbk.) | ISBN 9781978577145 (library bound) | ISBN 9781978577152 (ebook)
Subjects: LCSH: Forest ecology--Juvenile literature. | Forest animals--Juvenile literature. | Forest plants--Juvenile literature.
Classification: LCC QH541.5.F6 D65 2026 | DDC 577.3--dc23

Published in 2026 by
Norwood House Press
2544 Clinton Street
Buffalo, NY 14224

Designer: Rhea Magaro
Editor: Kim Thompson

Photo credits: Cover, p. 15 Inga Nielsen, Kumer Oksana/Shutterstock.com; p. 3 Ghxstwho/Shutterstock.com; p. 5 Ongala/Shutterstock.com; p. 6 olko1975/Shutterstock.com; p. 8 kato08/Shutterstock.com; p. 9 ADragan/Shutterstock.com; p. 11 Daleen Loest, shutter-tim82/Shutterstock.com; p. 12 Lukasz Gasiecki/Shutterstock.com; p. 13 Amy Lutz/Shutterstock.com; p. 15 Brad Doerksen /Shutterstock.com; p. 16 Bonnie Taylor Barry/Shutterstock.com; p. 18 roux pierre/Shutterstock.com; p. 19 S Byrne/Shutterstock.com; p. 20 GraphicsRF.com/Shutterstock.com; p. 21 Tillottama/Shutterstock.com

Printed in the United States of America

CPSIA compliance information: Batch #CWNHP26: For further information contact Norwood House Press at 1-800-237-9932.

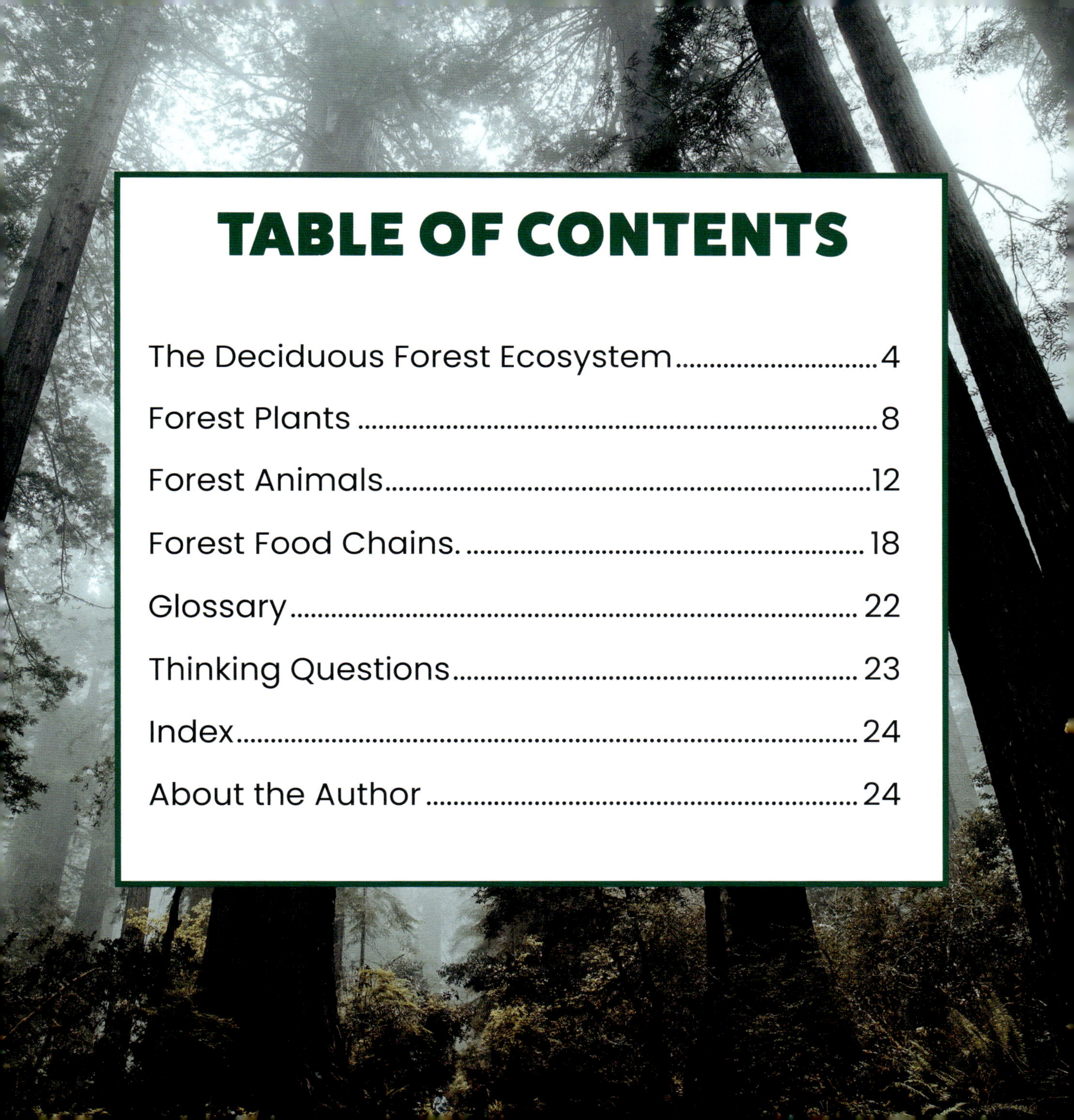

TABLE OF CONTENTS

The Deciduous Forest Ecosystem

Eco- means "home" or "environment." *System* means "a group of things that work together." Earth has many **ecosystems** that support life. Each is home to a network of living things that depend on each other.

One kind of ecosystem is a deciduous forest. A deciduous forest is full of trees that shed all their leaves each year in autumn and grow new leaves in the spring.

Deciduous forests grow in **temperate** places where there are four distinct seasons and where it rains or snows year-round. These forests are found in North America, Asia, and Europe.

Forest Plants

Special **adaptations** help plants grow in deciduous forests.

Oaks, maples, elms, and other trees have wide, thin leaves that **absorb** summer sunlight. In autumn, as the days get colder, the trees seal off each leaf's stem. **Chlorophyll**, which makes leaves green, breaks down. Red, gold, and orange colors emerge. After their leaves fall off, trees are better prepared to survive the winter. They lose less water and are protected from freezing temperatures.

In summer, the leaves of deciduous trees form a dense **canopy**. Not much sunlight reaches the forest floor.

In early spring, with no leaves overhead, wildflowers have a chance to bloom. Some kinds are trout lilies and wild columbines.

Forest Animals

Adaptations help animals live in leafy deciduous forests.

In autumn, squirrels and chipmunks gather and store nuts. The supply feeds them through winter as they huddle in their nests.

The black bear has a heavy coat with many layers of fur. Its long claws help it climb to safe places in hollow trees. Inside these trees or in other protected spaces, many black bears **hibernate** through the long, frozen winter.

Some animals spend only part of the year in deciduous forests. Ruby-throated hummingbirds spend the spring and summer in eastern North America. In autumn, they **migrate** to Mexico and Central America. Some fly 500 miles (800 kilometers) across the ocean.

Forest Food Chains

In a deciduous forest, living things eat other living things in food chains. A vole might eat seeds that fall from a tree. A garter snake may catch and eat the vole.

The garter snake might make a meal for a barred owl. After the owl dies, mushrooms and other **fungi** will help its body **decompose**.

Many forest food chains together form a food web. It shows how all living things in a deciduous forest ecosystem depend on each other for survival.

FOREST FOOD WEB

Glossary

absorb (ab-ZORB): to soak up or take in

adaptations (ad-ap-TAY-shuhns): physical or behavioral changes that help plants and animals survive in their environment

canopy (KAN-uh-pee): the uppermost, spreading, branching layer of a forest

chlorophyll (KLOR-uh-fil): the green pigment in plants that uses light to make food from carbon dioxide and water

decompose (dee-kuhm-POZE): to rot or decay and return nutrients to the soil

ecosystems (EE-koh-sis-tuhms): natural communities where plants, animals, and their environment all work together

fungi (FUHNG-gye): plant-like living things that have no leaves, roots, or flowers; mushrooms and molds are fungi

hibernate (HYE-bur-nate): to slow the heart rate and breathing and spend the winter in a still, sleep-like state

migrate (MYE-grate): to move from one place to another at a certain time of the year or to find food or other resources

temperate (TEM-pur-it): having temperatures that are rarely very high or very low

Thinking Questions

1. What is an ecosystem?
2. Where can you find deciduous forests on Earth?
3. Give an example of an adaptation that helps forest plants survive.
4. Give an example of an adaptation that helps forest animals survive.
5. What does a food chain show?

Index

About the Author

Francie Dolan is continually amazed by the natural world and how Earth's plants, animals, and natural resources are interconnected. From her home near Seattle, Washington, she loves to hike and explore forests, lakes, mountains, and the seashore. When she gets home, she likes to draw and write about what she sees on her adventures.